D1377177

Behind The Wheel™

Kurt Busch

NASCAR Driver

Jason Porterfield

rosen publishing's
rosen central®

New York

Published in 2007 by The Rosen Publishing Group, Inc.
29 East 21st Street, New York, NY 10010

First Edition

Library of Congress Cataloging-in-Publication Data

Porterfield, Jason.
Kurt Busch: NASCAR driver / Jason Porterfield. — 1st ed.
    p. cm. — (Behind the wheel)
Includes bibliographical references and index.
ISBN-13: 978-1-4042-0982-4
ISBN-10: 1-4042-0982-4 (library binding)
1. Busch, Kurt, 1978– 2. Automobile racing drivers — United States —
Biography — Juvenile literature. 3. Stock car racing — United
States — Juvenile literature. 4. Winston Cup — Juvenile literature.
I. Title. II. Series: Behind the wheel (Rosen Publishing Group)
GV1032.B89P67 2006
796.72092 — dc22
[B]
                                                    2006011083

Manufactured in the United States of America

On the cover: Kurt Busch sits in his #2 Miller Lite Dodge, on March 18, 2006.

CONTENTS

CHAPTER (1)

Born to Race

Upstart racing phenomenon Kurt Busch faced stiff competition as he entered the 2004 Ford 400 at the Homestead-Miami Speedway. One of the most successful drivers in the series, Busch had the points lead for the National Association of Stock Car Auto Racing's (NASCAR) inaugural Nextel Chase for the Cup. He would start the race as its leader, in the pole position.

Though Busch had been the points leader for ten weeks, his lead had nearly disappeared in the six races leading up to the Ford 400. Jimmie Johnson had won four of those races and was only sixteen points behind Busch. Jeff Gordon, Dale Earnhardt Jr., and Mark Martin were all within eighty-two points of the lead. The entire inaugural season of Nextel Chase for the Cup would be decided by this race, the last of the season.

Kurt Busch pulls his #97 Sharpie Ford into the pit area at Homestead-Miami Speedway during the Ford 400 on November 21, 2004. A problem with Busch's wheel nearly took him out of the race. Despite the setback, Busch finished the race in fifth place and captured the Nextel Cup Championship.

To win the series, Busch would have to finish in the top ten or better. More importantly, Johnson and Gordon could not win. Other upsets were also possible. Before NASCAR officials deducted points following a public outburst, Earnhardt had been the points leader. Busch's teammate Martin was a canny veteran driver who had never won the championship, though he

had placed second four times. Only eighty-two points behind, Martin also had an outside chance of winning the Nextel Cup. Over the course of the 271 laps that made up the 400-mile race (644 kilometers), the lead changed several times. Gordon, Earnhardt, and Johnson battled for position near the front, each hoping to take the lead and hold onto it to win the

Kurt Busch began the Ford 400 at Homestead-Miami Speedway on November 21, 2004, in first place. The day before a race, drivers run qualifying laps to determine the starting order for the next day's race.

championship. Further back, Martin slowly made his way toward the top ten. Meanwhile, Busch nearly wrecked when his right front wheel fell off, and at one point he fell back to twenty-eighth place before working his way back to the top five.

In the end, Busch's teammate Greg Biffle took the checkered flag, holding Johnson and Gordon off at the end. Johnson finished second, with Gordon right behind him in third. Busch finished fifth, winning the Nextel Cup by only eight points over Johnson, the narrowest margin ever.

Born to Race

Kurt Busch has racing in his blood. He was born in Las Vegas, Nevada, on August 4, 1978. His parents, Tom and Gaye Busch, had moved there from Chicago in 1977. They hoped to find relief for Gaye's arthritis in Las Vegas's dry desert climate.

Kurt and his younger brother, Kyle, born in 1985, grew up watching their father race. Tom started driving street stocks—ordinary cars customized for racing with strengthened frames and modified engines—the year that Kurt was born. Kurt spent much of his free time at the racetrack and in his father's garage, watching Tom work on his car. By the time he entered middle school, Kurt had decided that he also wanted to be a race car driver.

In 1991, Tom sold his stock car. He used the money to buy two miniature race cars called dwarf cars. Dwarf cars are replicas of classic automobiles built to five-eighths the size of the originals. The Buschs never allowed their sons to race go-karts competitively, which meant that the brothers started racing later in life than most other drivers.

Tom and Gaye Busch stand with their son before the NASCAR Nextel Cup Awards banquet. Kurt Busch is holding the Nextel Cup trophy, awarded to him after winning the 2004 Nextel Cup Championship. Prior to 2004, the series was known as the Winston Cup series.

Instead, Tom told Kurt that if he did well in school, he would be allowed to race the dwarf car when he turned sixteen. In the meantime, Tom resumed racing, winning the Nevada Dwarf Car Championship Series in 1994. Tom and Gaye Busch eventually relented—they allowed Kurt to begin racing dwarf cars in 1993, when he was just 14 years old. He showed enormous talent as a driver. In 1994, his father's championship year, Kurt was the runner-up in the series and won Rookie of the Year honors. He went on to win the Nevada Dwarf Car Championship Series in 1995.

Winning a championship in any racing division takes skill, patience, tenacity, and luck. Ultimately, winning depends on how many points a driver has earned. A driver is awarded a certain number of points based on what place he or she finishes. The driver finishing first receives the greatest number of points, and the driver finishing last receives the fewest. Most racing divisions have series, in which the points that drivers earn in each race are added in an ongoing tally. The driver with the most points at the end of the season wins the championship series.

The Next Step

Kurt Busch graduated from Las Vegas's Durango High School in 1996. That fall, he entered the University of Arizona. Motivated to find a cure for his mother's painful rheumatoid arthritis, Busch decided to pursue a degree in pharmacology. He continued racing in his spare time and built on his success in the Dwarf Car Series by entering other racing events. Busch began driving in the Legends Cars Series, once again racing five-eighths-scale reproductions of classic cars. He ultimately won the Legends Cars National Rookie of the Year Award in 1996, as well as the Legends Cars Western States Championship.

In addition to driving in the Legends Cars Series, he began driving a hobby stock car—a custom-built, full-size stock car placed on a regular car's chassis. He continued gathering awards throughout 1996 and into 1997, winning the NASCAR Hobby Stocks Rookie of the Year Award at Las Vegas Motor Speedway. He also successfully defended his Nevada Dwarf Car Championship Series crown. This ongoing success encouraged Busch to leave college and pursue racing full time.

DWARF CARS

Dwarf cars are replicas of 1928 to 1948 coupes and sedans built to five-eighths the size of the originals. They have an all-metal, fenderless body set on a chassis built by the Dwarf Car Company and are powered by motorcycle engines. The Dwarf Car Company was the brainchild of a man named Ernie Adams. Adams built the first prototype dwarf car for off-road racing through the desert outside of Phoenix, Arizona. He was soon commissioned to build more cars for local racing enthusiasts. In 1987, Adams formed the company with his friends John Cain and John Proctor.

Sponsorship

By 1998, Busch had turned his attention to full-size stock cars. He started driving in NASCAR's Featherlite Southwest Tour that year.

Featherlite, the sponsor of the Southwest Tour, is a company that manufactures aluminum transport trailers. By sponsoring the racing series, Featherlite made its company name instantly recognizable to thousands of fans.

Companies like Featherlite pay team owners to have their name and logo painted on cars driven through all levels of racing. In a local series, sponsors as diverse as garages, hotels, large farms, and even local political candidates pay for this kind of advertising. Sponsors for teams on the higher-level Busch Grand National and Nextel Cup series tend to be national corporations or organizations such as grocery store chains and snack food companies.

Drivers often have dozens of sponsor logos on their cars, with the largest and most prominent going to the highest bidder. Sponsoring a successful driver can generate revenue and introduce new consumers to a company's product or service. Team owners, in turn, usually pay their drivers' expenses and generate revenue through arrangements with automakers and outside sponsorship deals.

When Busch joined the Featherlite Southwest Series, he signed a contract to drive for a racing team owned by Craig Keough. The team was sponsored by Star Nursery, Keough's own Las Vegas–based company. As the team's proprietor, Keough owned the race car and its components, as well as extra cars, tools, replacement parts, and the garage in which to store and repair them. Busch and several other drivers signed contracts to race cars for Keough. Busch would drive a late-model stock car very similar to those used in NASCAR's Busch Grand National and Winston Cup series.

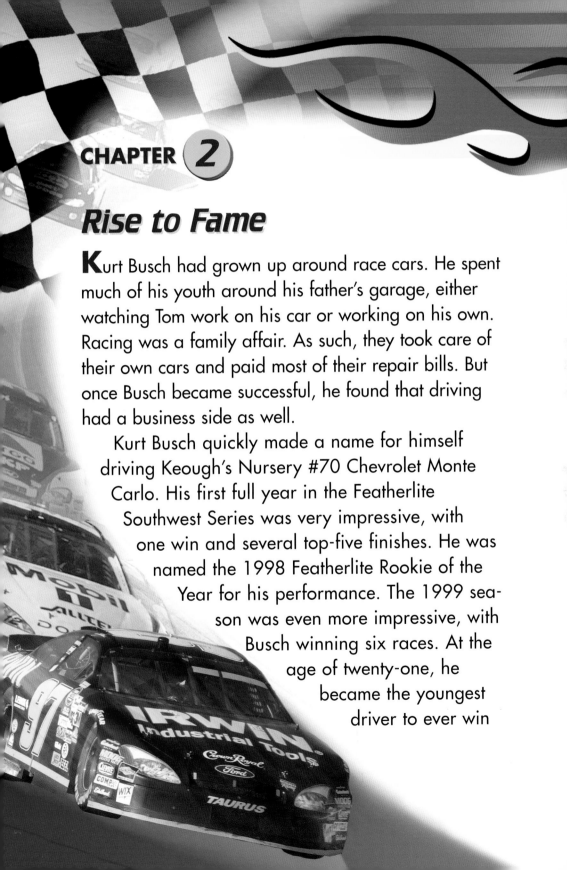

CHAPTER 2

Rise to Fame

Kurt Busch had grown up around race cars. He spent much of his youth around his father's garage, either watching Tom work on his car or working on his own. Racing was a family affair. As such, they took care of their own cars and paid most of their repair bills. But once Busch became successful, he found that driving had a business side as well.

Kurt Busch quickly made a name for himself driving Keough's Nursery #70 Chevrolet Monte Carlo. His first full year in the Featherlite Southwest Series was very impressive, with one win and several top-five finishes. He was named the 1998 Featherlite Rookie of the Year for his performance. The 1999 season was even more impressive, with Busch winning six races. At the age of twenty-one, he became the youngest driver to ever win

Jack Roush is the founder and owner of Roush Racing, one of NASCAR's most successful racing teams. The owner of an engineering firm, he has fielded NASCAR teams since 1988, when he began working with driver Mark Martin. Roush was inducted into the International Motorsports Hall of Fame on April 27, 2006.

the Featherlite Series Championship.

Driver X

Racing team owner Jack Roush was among the thousands of fans who saw Busch drive that season. Roush invited Busch to try out for his racing team in a special contest called the Driver X Tryout. He held these auditions whenever he needed a new driver. Busch's was one of five invitations Roush extended that year as he searched for a new driver for his Craftsman Truck racing team. He set up a series of three tryouts for his prospective drivers.

Busch was nervous for the first test, held in Toledo, Ohio. Though he avoided making major mistakes in the tryout, he also failed to distinguish himself from the other drivers. The second tryout went far better for Busch. Roush had changed the setup and format of the tryout, and Busch adjusted quickly and calmly to the new circumstances. Roush was greatly impressed by Busch's driving.

Those who auditioned also had to conduct mock interviews to demonstrate their ability to handle the media. Busch performed well in that respect, demonstrating his intelligence and poise. The third tryout was merely a formality. After its completion, Roush offered Kurt Busch a contract to drive for Roush Racing—a contract that would eventually lead to a NASCAR championship.

NASCAR's Wild Ride

When Kurt Busch joined Roush Racing, he was following a path laid out for him by generations of drivers. Stock car racing began developing during the Prohibition era of the late 1920s and early 1930s. At the time, it was a federal crime to make, sell, or possess alcohol. People called bootleggers made alcohol in defiance of the law. They paid drivers to load their cars with illegal whiskey and drive it into major cities and towns. Most of these trips were undertaken at night on the back roads of the American Southeast, as the drivers sought to outrun federal authorities and deliver their cargo. The whiskey runners, called whiskey trippers, took pride in their fast cars and their ability to maneuver sharp curves. They began getting together and racing each other in loosely organized local contests.

15

Several governing bodies grew up to organize these races, though the only one to survive was NASCAR, which formed in 1947. Only street-stock cars—cars that had been unmodified for speed or maneuverability—were allowed to enter early NASCAR races.

Today, the cars are custom built, and only the body resembles that of a "pure" stock car. By the 1970s, NASCAR's premier racing series was sponsored by the R. J. Reynolds Tobacco Company. It became known as the Winston Cup Series. The Grand National became the second-highest division and was sponsored by Busch beer.

By the beginning of the twenty-first century, NASCAR was the third most popular spectator sport in the United States after football and basketball. The sport's increasing popularity and visibility brought NASCAR to end its longtime affiliation with R. J. Reynolds in 2003 in favor of a less controversial sponsor. The telecommunications company Nextel took over in 2004, renaming the series the Nextel Chase for the Cup. The point system of the series was altered when Nextel became its sponsor. Fewer points would separate a first-place finish from a tenth-place finish, keeping the points race closer throughout the season. The top ten points leaders would then compete in the Chase, which takes place over the last ten races of the season. The winner of the Chase would win the cup. Other drivers would still race, but they would be out of contention for the Nextel Cup.

During the 1950s, NASCAR's top series was called the Grand National. Many races remained informal and loosely organized, such as the "Flying Mile" stock car race held at Daytona Speedway. Organizers marked off the course on the beach itself, rather than on a track. Here, driver Danny Eames is shown winning 1956's "Flying Mile" in his Dodge D-500.

Contract and Controversy

Busch signed a contract to spend the 2000 season driving for Roush in the Craftsman Truck Series. Begun in 1995, it is a relatively new racing series. Craftsman drivers race modified Ford, Chevrolet, and Dodge trucks capable of reaching speeds of more than 180 miles per hour (290 kilometers per hour). Most truck races take place on short tracks, with each lap covering a little more than one mile (1.6 km). The truck series usually functions as an additional proving ground for drivers before they graduate to the Busch Grand National Series.

Roush had Busch drive the #99 Ford, sponsored by Exide Batteries. Despite Busch's youth, Roush felt he was ready to compete in a national racing series. At Dover International Speedway, in Dover, Delaware, he set a record for being the youngest driver to ever start a Craftsman Truck race in the pole position. By winning that race, he established another record by becoming the youngest driver to ever win a race in the series. Busch ultimately won four races in the 2000 Craftsman Truck Series, placed in the top five in ten more, and finished second in points. At the end of the season, he was named Rookie of the Year.

Driving in the Winston Cup

In addition to driving in the Craftsman Truck Series, Busch started in seven Winston Cup races, driving the #97 Ford sponsored by John Deere. Roush created a stir within the NASCAR community by allowing Busch to drive in these races without first racing in the Busch Grand National Series, considered by many to be a training ground for the Winston Cup Series. Other drivers and team owners thought Busch was too young and unproven to race in the Winston Cup Series. Despite this controversy, Kurt Busch's debut did not attract much attention. His Winston Cup races that season were unremarkable, and the young driver worked to adjust to his car and the high-caliber competition. He

Kurt Busch is shown behind the wheel of his #97 Sharpie Ford at Virginia's Martinsville Speedway before practicing for the 2002 Virginia 500. Busch started the Virginia 500 in 20th position and ultimately finished the race in tenth place. The strong finish put him in fourth place in the Winston Cup standings.

never started any higher than tenth place or finished higher than thirteenth.

The Rookie

Kurt Busch's performance in the Craftsman Truck Series and his composure throughout his seven Winston Cup races impressed Jack Roush. In 2001, Roush made Busch a full-time Winston Cup driver. Busch would be joining

A pack of trucks start the 2005 Silverado 350 at Texas Motor Speedway. In 1993, a group of racers designed and built the first racing pickup truck. NASCAR introduced the Super Trucks Series a couple years later, changing its name to the Craftsman Truck Series in 1996. Since its creation, the series has proven popular with both young drivers and veteran racers.

one of NASCAR's elite Winston Cup teams. Roush's other Winston Cup drivers included respected veteran racers Mark Martin and Jeff Burton, who gave Busch guidance during his first races and throughout 2001.

Busch quickly improved on his 2000 Winston Cup experience. He earned a reputation among his Roush team members and crew as being a respectful driver, a quick learner, and someone who's eager to listen to advice. Once again, he drove the #97 John Deere Ford. Through the season, he started in thirty-six races, though he failed to finish seven of them. He didn't win any races, but he finished in the top five three times and had six finishes in the top ten.

On September 2, 2001, Busch won the pole position for the Mountain Dew Southern 500 at Darlington Raceway, in Darlington, South Carolina. Busch ultimately finished far back in the pack in the thirty-ninth position, but capturing the pole was an important milestone for him. He finished the 2001 season twenty-seventh in the standings, a respectable position for a young rookie. He came in second to Kevin Harvick in the voting for NASCAR's Rookie of the Year. Heading into the off-season, Busch resolved to work even harder the next year.

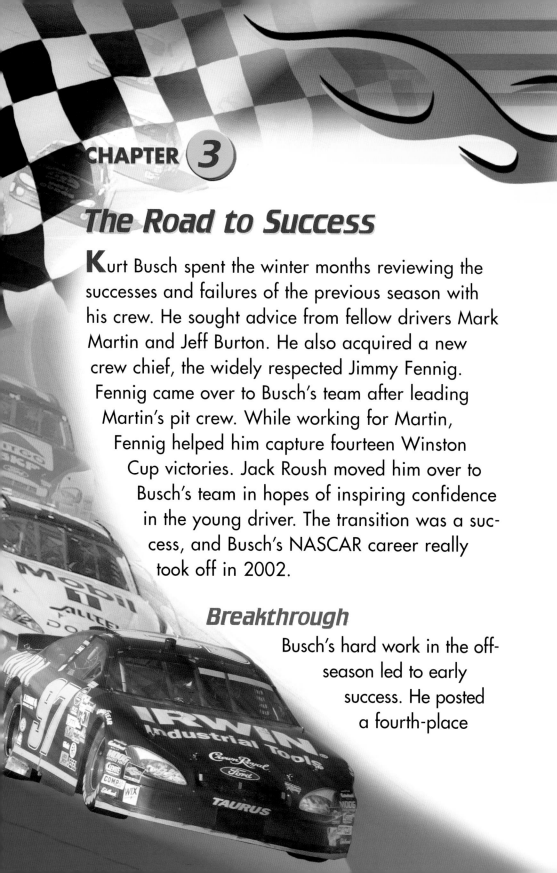

CHAPTER 3

The Road to Success

Kurt Busch spent the winter months reviewing the successes and failures of the previous season with his crew. He sought advice from fellow drivers Mark Martin and Jeff Burton. He also acquired a new crew chief, the widely respected Jimmy Fennig. Fennig came over to Busch's team after leading Martin's pit crew. While working for Martin, Fennig helped him capture fourteen Winston Cup victories. Jack Roush moved him over to Busch's team in hopes of inspiring confidence in the young driver. The transition was a success, and Busch's NASCAR career really took off in 2002.

Breakthrough

Busch's hard work in the off-season led to early success. He posted a fourth-place

Kurt Busch talks with his crew chief Jimmy Fennig before the 2004 Ford 400. Fennig spent several successful years as crew chief for NASCAR legend Bobby Allison's team, Bobby Allison Motorsports, and joined Roush Racing in 1996 as Mark Martin's crew chief. He was Busch's crew chief from 2001 to 2005.

finish in the Daytona 500 before enduring four races without even a top-ten finish. This drought ended at the Food City 500, held on March 24, 2002, at Bristol Motor Speedway in Bristol, Tennessee. Driving the #97 Rubbermaid/Sharpie Ford, Busch started the race back

Racing at the 2002 Food City 500 at Bristol Motor Speedway, Kurt Busch's #97 Sharpie Ford moves to the outside to pass the #15 NAPA Auto Parts Chevrolet driven by Michael Waltrip. Busch went on to win the race, making it his first Winston Cup victory.

at the 27th position. He gradually worked his way up into the top ten through careful management of caution flags and pit stops, taking over the lead on the 413th lap and holding onto it through the rest of the race. This brought Busch up to fifth place in the Winston Cup standings.

Busch's success continued through the following weeks as he moved up toward the top of the rankings. He posted three top-ten finishes over the next five races, going on to participate in the Winston Cup, a 90-lap, all-star event held in May. Busch finished in fourth place, but got into trouble with NASCAR officials over some inappropriate comments he made after the race.

Busch's position in the Winston Cup standings slipped over the summer, but he managed to stay in the top ten. Finishing in the top ten for five out of six races spanning June and July, he also earned a second-place finish in the Pennsylvania 500 at Pocono Raceway. Busch went through three consecutive late-summer races in which he did not finish, but he overcame these problems late in the season. He won two consecutive races in October, the Old Dominion 500 and the Napa 500, and won the final race of the season, the Ford 400. Busch consistently placed in the top ten, including ten of the season's final twelve races. He finished the season in third place in the Winston Cup standings with 4,641 points. This put him 159 points

PIT CREW

A driver's skill is not the only factor in building a successful racing team. Owners and drivers need excellent pit crews to repair and maintain their cars. The crews work both in the pit area of a racetrack and in the garage. In the pit, each crew member is part of a smaller team with specialized jobs. One team changes tires, while another refuels the car. Other team members check fluids, look for mechanical problems, repair any damage done to the car's body, and see to the driver's needs. Because they work during races, pit crews must do their jobs quickly under pressure. The seconds spent changing tires and straightening bent sheet metal can mean the difference between finishing in the top five or out of the top ten.

behind Winston Cup winner Tony Stewart and 121 points behind runner-up Mark Martin. He had won four races, placed in the top five 12 times, and the top ten 20 times. His earnings for the season totaled just over $5 million.

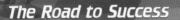

Kurt Busch makes a pit stop at the 2001 Sharpie 500 during his rookie season as a NASCAR driver. He eventually finished the season as the runner-up for NASCAR's Rookie of the Year award. By winning the 2004 Nextel Cup Championship, Busch proved he was one of NASCAR's premier drivers.

A Frustrating Season

Kurt Busch had a phenomenal year in 2002. Expectations for the 2003 Winston Cup season were very high. He started out well, placing second in the first two races of the year: the Daytona 500 and the Subway 400. After this promising beginning, Busch failed to finish the next two races. His car was knocked out of the UAW-DaimlerChrysler 400 by an accident with eighty-eight

Kurt Busch talks with a crew member after practicing for an upcoming race at New Hampshire International Speedway. Practices give drivers and crews the opportunity to fine-tune their cars before the race. Drivers communicate with their pit crews throughout races, discussing strategy and the race car's condition.

laps remaining. His chances for winning the Bass Pro Shops MBNA 500 were shot when engine trouble forced him to quit the race on his 144th lap.

Busch's luck seemed to improve somewhat after the MBNA 500. He placed second in the Carolina Dodge Dealers 400, which took place the next weekend at Darlington Raceway. He won his first race of the year, the Food City 500, on March 23 at Bristol. A month later, he won the Auto Club 500 at California Speedway in Fontana, California. His third victory of the season came at the Sirius 400 at Michigan International Speedway in Brooklyn, Michigan.

Busch's season hit a lull after that, and then disaster struck in a race at Michigan International Speedway. He started the race 20th and finished 18th. Busch had the lead going into the final laps when he had to make a pit stop for fuel with only a lap to go. As he attempted to make his way back to the front, his #97 Ford and Jimmy Spencer's car bumped each other several times.

When the race ended and the drivers headed to the garage, Busch's car stopped in front of Spencer's transport trailer. Spencer rammed the back of Busch's car and walked around to the driver's side window, where he leaned in and struck Busch in the face. Busch climbed out of his car and yelled at Spencer, but no more blows were exchanged.

Busch went to the track's medical center to have his face examined. Afterwards, the two drivers and their crew chiefs met with NASCAR officials to tell their sides of the story. According to Spencer, Busch had parked his car in front of Spencer's and revved the engine while yelling at the older driver. Busch claimed that his car had simply run out of gas and that Spencer had not been provoked in any way. After the meeting, Spencer refused to talk about the confrontation. Busch insisted that the bumping between the cars had been unintentional and only came about because both drivers had been racing hard. In the days that followed, however, transcripts of radio conversations that had taken place between Busch and Fennig during the race told a different story. According to the transcripts, Busch talked to his crew about wanting to hit Spencer's #7 Dodge.

Busch was criticized by fans and the media after the transcripts were released, while Spencer was praised for showing restraint until after the race. Busch had already been fined by NASCAR twice in 2002. He and Spencer had feuded in the past. NASCAR penalized both drivers after the Michigan incident, suspending Spencer for a race and placing both on probation for the rest of the season.

Busch bounced back in his next race, winning the Sharpie 500, but the rest of his 2003 season went poorly. He only had three top-ten finishes after August—and only finished in the top five once. He also failed to finish in four late-season races. Though he ended the season with four wins, nine top-five finishes, and fourteen total top tens, he did not complete a career-high eight races. Busch's team closed out the season with an 11th-place ranking in the Winston Cup standings, a huge disappointment after 2002.

The Nextel Cup

At the end of the 2003 season, Kurt Busch's popularity had taken a serious blow. Fans and reporters remembered his part in the incident at Michigan and were reluctant to forgive him. His reputation among other drivers had changed as well. Some now considered him hotheaded and arrogant. In addition to Spencer, Busch had feuded with Terry Labonte and Sterling Marlin.

Busch entered the 2004 season determined to change people's minds. That year, the series sponsor was changed from R. J. Reynolds Tobacco to Nextel. The Winston Cup was now the Nextel Cup, a move designed to improve NASCAR's image among its growing fan base. The series would include a ten-race chase at the end of the season, in which the top-ten points leaders would compete directly for the Nextel Cup. Busch got off to an excellent start, with six top-ten finishes in his first eight races before winning the Food City 500 for the third year in a row. He continued to drive well throughout the year.

Though he won only three races in 2004, he had ten top-five finishes and finished in the top ten 21 times. During the ten races of the chase itself, he had six top-five finishes, including a win in the Sylvania 300 at Watkins Glen International, in Watkins Glen, New York. He led all Nextel drivers in points throughout the last eight races. When the season ended, Busch had an eight-point lead over second-place driver Jimmie Johnson. Busch was declared the first winner of the Nextel Cup with the closest points total in NASCAR history. Almost as important, he avoided controversy throughout the season. Slowly but surely, Busch's image was improving.

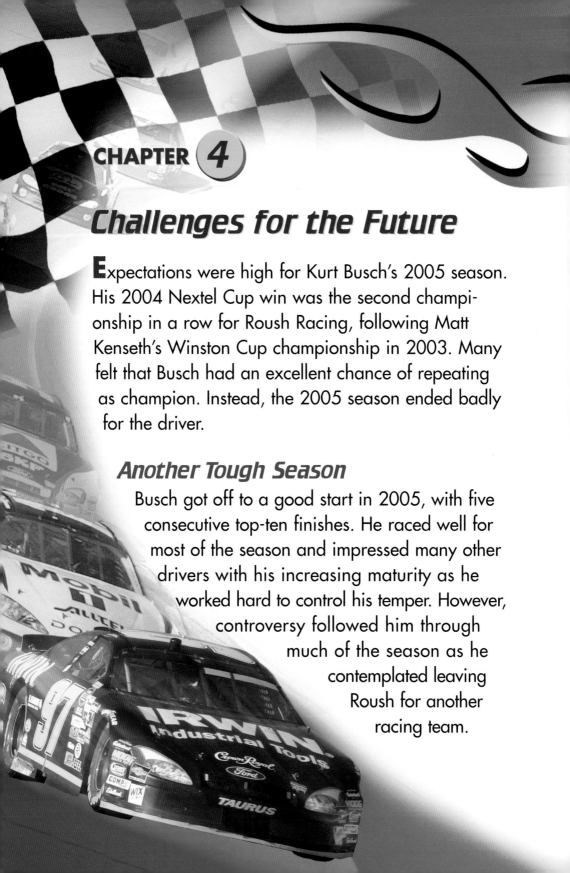

CHAPTER ④

Challenges for the Future

Expectations were high for Kurt Busch's 2005 season. His 2004 Nextel Cup win was the second championship in a row for Roush Racing, following Matt Kenseth's Winston Cup championship in 2003. Many felt that Busch had an excellent chance of repeating as champion. Instead, the 2005 season ended badly for the driver.

Another Tough Season

Busch got off to a good start in 2005, with five consecutive top-ten finishes. He raced well for most of the season and impressed many other drivers with his increasing maturity as he worked hard to control his temper. However, controversy followed him through much of the season as he contemplated leaving Roush for another racing team.

Kurt Busch, Mark Martin, and Scott Riggs collide at Daytona International Speedway during the Pepsi 400 on July 2, 2005. Though wrecks frequently knock drivers out of the competition, all three drivers managed to complete the race.

The popular driver Rusty Wallace, of Penske Racing, planned to retire at the end of the season, leaving his #2 Miller Lite Dodge without a driver. Team owner Roger Penske, impressed with Kurt Busch's championship season, invited him to join the team. In August, Busch announced he would leave Roush Racing when his contract expired at the end of 2006 and drive Wallace's car for Penske in 2007. He would also seek an early release from his contract with Roush in order to join Penske in 2006. Despite the distraction of contract negotiations, he won three races, with nine top-five and eighteen top-ten finishes. Busch easily qualified for the chase and was fifth in the standings to leader Tony Stewart as the chase began.

Busch trailed Stewart in the standings by only 20 points before the Sylvania 300, the first of the ten races to determine the championship. He had just won the Chevy 500 the week before and was starting the race in 12th position. A messy wreck with driver Scott Riggs destroyed Busch's car, however. Busch reacted poorly in the pit area, yelling at Riggs's crew chief. He eventually finished 35th. When the race ended, Busch had dropped to tenth in the standings, 142 points behind Stewart.

Though he never came closer to Stewart in points, Busch managed to climb into eighth place in the standings before causing another public-relations dis-aster. On November 17, he was pulled over by police near Phoenix, Arizona, on suspicion of drunken driv-ing. A Breathalyzer test indicated that his blood alcohol level was well below the legal limit, but he was still charged with reckless driving. Reports indicated that he argued with the officer before taking the sobriety test, and that he was briefly detained by police. Roush

Racing suspended Busch for the final two races of the season and cut its ties with the driver. Denied a chance to finish the season, Busch dropped to tenth place in the standings as Tony Stewart wrapped up his second championship.

Even as his hopes for winning another championship faded and his season fell apart, Busch could take some pleasure in watching his younger brother, Kyle, a member of the Hendrick Motorsports racing team and driver of the #5 Kellogg's Chevrolet Monte Carlo. It was Kyle's rookie season in the Nextel Cup Series. He drove well, winning two races and becoming the youngest driver to ever win a race at NASCAR's highest level. Kyle was eventually named the Nextel Rookie of the Year.

A Fresh Start

The run-in with police did not change Kurt Busch's relationship with Penske Racing. Team owner Roger Penske stood by Busch as his newest driver faced a new wave of public criticism. Penske confirmed that Busch would begin the 2006 season behind the wheel of the #2 Miller Lite Dodge Charger. On February 8, 2006, Busch made a court appearance for the November traffic stop, pleading guilty to speeding, passing illegally, and following too closely behind another vehicle. He was ordered to perform fifty hours of community service within a year and pay $580 in fines.

In the aftermath of the incident, Busch focused on the upcoming season, preparing to make the switch to his new team. Taking over Rusty Wallace's #2 Miller Lite Dodge required him to learn how to handle a different car from the Fords he had driven for Roush. Busch also had to become acquainted with an entirely new pit crew. His new crew chief, Roy McCauley, had worked with

Driving the #2 Miller Lite Dodge, Kurt Busch starts the 2006 Auto Club 500 in the pole position at the California Speedway in Fontana, California. The pole position—referring to the first-place position at a race's start—goes to the driver with the fastest qualifying laps.

Penske driver Ryan Newman on the Busch Grand National circuit. Busch relied heavily on McCauley for advice on handling the Dodge as he prepared for the season's opening races. With McCauley's help and

Penske's support, Busch had yet another chance to regain his championship form.

Off the Track

Busch expects to make some substantial changes in his personal life during the 2006 season. In July 2005, he became engaged to his longtime girlfriend, Eva Bryan. The two met on a blind date in 2003 and have been together ever since. They plan to live in Charlotte, North Carolina, where Busch bought a house in 2002. He moved there from Las Vegas because of its close proximity to many racetracks. The move allows him to spend a greater portion of his time at home during the season. Busch's parents live nearby.

When he's not racing, Busch loves to play golf and has participated in a number of charity golfing events. He's an avid fan of the Chicago Cubs baseball team, and in 2004 and 2005, he took part in the Racin' the Bases Celebrity Softball Game. The game raised money for NASCAR's Victory Junction Gang Camp, a camp for children with chronic or life-threatening illnesses and their families. Busch was thrilled to play alongside Cubs Hall-of-Fame second baseman Ryne Sandberg, a player he had admired while growing up.

Busch also has a hand in several other charities. In 2004, his championship year, he joined Rebuilding Together. Rebuilding Together is a nationwide organization

Kurt Busch celebrates his victory in the Food City 500 at Bristol Motor Speedway on March 26, 2006. The win was his first as the driver of Penske Racing's #2 Miller Lite Dodge, driven in previous seasons by NASCAR legend Rusty Wallace. Wallace retired at the end of the 2005 season, ending a career that spanned 25 years.

that is committed to renovating and remodeling older buildings for low-income families. By joining, Busch helped to draw the public's attention to the organization, which rebuilds or refurbishes more than 8,000 homes and community centers each year.

The Future

Kurt Busch is far from the only NASCAR driver to get in trouble for having a short temper. Though some fans may not remember, Rusty Wallace was also considered hotheaded and outspoken when he first appeared on the Winston Cup circuit. Despite the controversies that have followed him throughout his career, Busch has shown himself to be one of the most talented young drivers in NASCAR. However, he has a lot of work ahead of him in 2006.

As the driver of the #2 Miller Lite car, Busch will join a team with a long history of winning. His predecessor, Rusty Wallace, won 55 races and became a legend while driving the same car. With 14 career wins and a Nextel Cup championship by the age of 27, Busch seems poised to follow in Wallace's footsteps.

Awards

1994 Nevada State Dwarf Car Rookie of the Year

Las Vegas Motor Speedway Dwarf Car Points Champion

1995 Nevada State Dwarf Car Champion

Las Vegas Motor Speedway Dwarf Car Points Champion

1996 Legends Cars Western States Champion

Legends Cars National Rookie of the Year

NASCAR Hobby Stocks Champion

1998 Featherlite Southwest Series Rookie of the Year

1999 Featherlite Southwest Series Champion

2004 NASCAR Nextel Cup Champion

Glossary

aerodynamic Describes an object that is designed to move at high speeds without creating wind resistance.

Breathalyzer A device used to determine the amount of alcohol in a person's bloodstream.

chassis A steel frame that forms the skeleton of an automobile.

circuit An established set of places or events visited by a particular group of people.

coupe A car with a closed top and two doors; coupes often have no rear seat.

drag The creation of resistance to movement, slowing progress.

dwarf car A race car built on a five-eighths scale and designed to resemble a classic automobile.

lap One circuit around a race course.

off-season In sports, the part of the year between the end of one season and the beginning of another.

pharmacology The science and study of drugs and their uses and effects.

pit The center area of a racetrack, usually bounded by the track itself.

pole position The best position at the start of a race.

prototype An early model.

rheumatoid arthritis A disease causing painful swelling in the joints.

rookie An inexperienced person; someone new to a job or sport.

sedan A car with two to four doors and a closed top.

sponsor A business, organization, or individual that supports an effort or endeavor.

stock car A race car with the same basic chassis of a car available to the public.

tenacity Persistent determination.

For More Information

NASCAR
301 South College Street, Suite 3900
Charlotte, NC 28202
(704) 348-9600
Web site: http://www.nascar.com

Penske Racing
200 Penske Way
Mooresville, NC 28115
(704) 664-2300
Web site: http://www.penskeracing.com

Roush Racing
11851 Market Street
Livonia, MI 48150
(734) 779-7291
Web site: http://www.roushracing.com

Web Sites

Due to the changing nature of Internet links, Rosen Publishing has developed an online list of Web sites related to the subject of this book. This site is updated regularly. Please use this link to access the list:

http://www.rosenlinks.com/bw/kubu

For Further Reading

Bentley, Ross. *Speed Secrets: Professional Race Driving Techniques.* Osceola, WI: MBI Publishing Company, 1998.

Cothren, Larry. *NASCAR's Next Generation.* St. Paul, MN: Crestline, 2003.

Fresina, Michael J. *A Week in the Life of NASCAR: A View from Within.* Chicago, IL: Triumph Books, 2005.

Fresina, Michael J. *For the Love of NASCAR: An A-to-Z Primer for NASCAR Fans of All Ages.* Chicago, IL: Triumph Books, 2005.

Higgins, Tom. *NASCAR Greatest Races: The 25 Most Thrilling Races in NASCAR History.* New York, NY: HarperCollins Publishers, 1999.

Hunter, Don, and Ben White. *NASCAR Legends.* St. Paul, MN: Crestline, 2004.

NASCAR Record & Fact Book: 2006 Edition. St. Louis, MO: Sporting News, 2006.

Bibliography

Anderson, Lars. "Bumper cars." *Sports Illustrated*, Vol. 103, No. 12, September 26, 2005, p. 31.

Associated Press. "Kurt Busch on the Road to Recovery." *St. Petersburg Times*. April 25, 2005. Retrieved February 20, 2006 (http://www.sptimes.com/2005/04/25/Sports/Kurt_Busch_on_the_roa.shtml).

Bradley, Mark. "A New Chapter in the Book of Busch." Cox News Service. January 22, 2006. Retrieved February 20, 2006 (http://www.joliet.com/joliet/raceways/chicagoland/news/2_7_AU22_BUSCH_S1html).

Gladden, Rebecca. "Kurt Busch Can't Win." InsiderRacingNews.com. November 26, 2004. Retrieved February 20, 2006 (http://insiderracingnews.com/RG/112604.html).

Hagstrom, Robert G. *The NASCAR Way: The Business that Drives the Sport*. New York, NY: John Wiley & Sons, Inc., 1998.

Hemphill, Paul. *Wheels: A Season on NASCAR's Winston Cup Circuit*. New York, NY: Simon and Schuster, 1997.

James, Brant. "Mining for the Good Kurt Busch." *St. Petersburg Times*. November 21, 2004. Retrieved February 20, 2006 (http://www.sptimes.com/2004/11/21/Sports/Mining_for_the_good_K.shtml).

Long, Dustin. "Dad's Real Driver in Busch Title Chases." *Virginian-Pilot*. October 19, 2004. Retrieved February 20, 2006 (http://home.hamptonroads.com/stories/story.cfm?story=76952&ran=117138).

Menzer, Joe. *The Wildest Ride: A History of NASCAR*. New York, NY: Simon and Schuster, 2001.

Minter, Rick. "NASCAR: Controversy-Prone Busch Vows to Leave Past in Dust." *Atlanta Journal-Constitution*. January 19, 2006, p. D.11.

Minter, Rick. "From Stewart's Reinvention to Kurt Busch's Woes: A Look at the Highs and Lows of Year 2 of the Chase for the Nextel Cup." *Atlanta Journal-Constitution*. November 21, 2005. Retrieved February 20, 2006 (http://www.ajc.com/sports/content/shared/sports/racing/stories/1121nascar_notes.html).

NASCAR Press Release. "Car of Tomorrow to Make Race Debut in 2007." NASCAR.com. January 23, 2006. Retrieved February 20, 2006 (http://www.nascar.com/2006/news/headlines/cup/01/ 23/car.of.tomorrow.begins.2 007/index.html).

Roush Racing. "Kurt Busch 97." Roush Racing.com. Retrieved February 20, 2006 (http://www.roushracing.com/Kurt_Busch/ default.asp?page=/kurt_busch/kbbio.htm).

Roush Racing. "Kurt Busch—archives, 2000–2006." Roush Racing.com. Retrieved February 20, 2006 (http:// www.roushracing.com/Kurt_Busch/default.asp?page=/ kurt_busch/archive.a sp).

Smith, Marty. "In Review: Kurt Busch." NASCAR.com. December 13, 2005. Retrieved February 20, 2006 (http://www.nascar.com/ 2005/news/headlines/cup/12/13/kbusch_yir/index.html).

Smithson, Ryan. "Roush: Busch 'Used Up His Equity' With Team." NASCAR.com. November 18, 2005. Retrieved February 20, 2006 (http://www.nascar.com/2005/news/headlines/cup/11/18/ kbusch.jroush.miami/inde x.html).

Woody, Larry. "Jekyll and Hyde: Kurt Busch's Personality May Oscillate Between Timid and Temperamental, but He's a Monster Talent." *Auto Racing Digest*, December 2002.

Index

About The Author

Jason Porterfield is a freelance writer and researcher living in Chicago. He is the author of more than 15 books for Rosen, on subjects ranging from American history to environmental science. He has also written biographies of Annie Oakley and the French author and philosopher Voltaire. Jason grew up in the mountains of Virginia, where he often heard stories about the bootleggers and whisky runners who laid the foundations of NASCAR. While writing this book, he was completely drawn into Kurt Busch's story and his place in recent NASCAR history.

Photo Credits

Cover, pp. 1,14 Chris Stanford/Getty Images; p. 1 © Doug Pensinger/ Getty Images; pp. 5, 27 © Robert Laberge/Getty Images; pp. 6–7, 23, 39 © Rusty Jarrett/Getty Images; pp. 9, 19 © Jamie Squire/Getty Images for NASCAR; p.17 © Walter Bennett/Time & Life Pictures/Getty Images; pp. 20, 24 © Jonathan Ferrey/Getty Images; p. 28 © Joel Page/AP Photo; p. 33 © Glenn Smith/AP Photo; pp. 36–37 © Todd Warshaw/ Getty Images.

Designer: Gene Mollica